The Teachings of Gandhi: 300 days of Inspiration and Growth

By Mahatma Gandhi
&
Daniel Willey

ISBN-13: 978-1494918903
ISBN-10: 1494918900

All rights reserved.
Published by Easy Publishing Company
http://www.easypublishingcompany.com
contact@easypublishingcompany.com
Salt Lake City, UT 84108

First Edition: January 2014
Printed in the United States of America

Table of Contents

Ways to Use this Book:

1. Start your day by reading a quote. Start at number 1 and read one quote per day. Write the quote down and share it throughout your day with others.
2. Buy a journal and record your responses to each of the quotes. Write down your feelings, thoughts, and inspirations.
3. Read this book as you would read any other book, from beginning to end.
4. Pick a random number, 1-365, then find and read that quote. Use it on days or at times when you need extra inspiration.

Introduction

Mohandas Karamchand Gandhi was the preeminent leader and freedom fighter of Indian nationalism in British-ruled India. Employing nonviolent civil disobedience, Gandhi led India to independence and inspired movements for civil rights and freedom across the world. The honorific Mahatma is now used worldwide. He is also called Bapu in India.

I have always considered quotes to be a very valuable asset to my inspiration. For years I have scoured the web to find meaningful quotes from inspirational people. When I find an especially meaningful quote, I love to share it with those close to me. I think that when you share something special to yourself, it can become even more meaningful and help out others.

NOTE: The Quotes in this book are collected from many sources and time periods. To respect the integrity of the authors' work, I have made every reasonable effort to correctly attribute each quote to the original author, but in a few cases it was impossible to find the exact original quote. I have made every effort to give credit to the person who first spoke the classic version of each quote.

1

"Be the change that you wish to see in the world."

2

"Live as if you were to die tomorrow. Learn as if you were to live forever."

3

"An eye for an eye will only make the whole world blind."

4

"Happiness is when what you think, what you say, and what you do are in harmony."

5

"The weak can never forgive. Forgiveness is the attribute of the strong."

6
"Seven Deadly Sins:
Wealth without work
Pleasure without conscience
Science without humanity
Knowledge without character
Politics without principle
Commerce without morality
Worship without sacrifice."

7
"When I despair, I remember that all through history the way of truth and love have always won. There have been tyrants and murderers, and for a time, they

can seem invincible, but in the end, they always fall. Think of it-- always."

8

"First they ignore you, then they ridicule you, then they fight you, and then you win."

9

"Where there is love there is life."

10

"I like your Christ, I do not like your Christians. Your Christians are so unlike your Christ."

11

"Freedom is not worth having if it does not include the freedom to make mistakes."

12
"Nobody can hurt me without my permission."

13
"Prayer is not asking. It is a longing of the soul. It is daily admission of one's weakness. It is better in prayer to have a heart without words than words without a heart."

14
"God has no religion."

15

"Hate the sin, love the sinner."

16
"I will not let anyone walk through my mind with their dirty feet."

17
"A man is but the product of his thoughts. What he thinks, he becomes."

18
"To give pleasure to a single heart by a single act is better than a thousand heads bowing in prayer."

19

"Earth provides enough to satisfy every man's needs, but not every man's greed."

20
"The best way to find yourself is to lose yourself in the service of others."

21
"The future depends on what you do today."

22
"You must not lose faith in humanity. Humanity is like an ocean; if a few drops of the ocean are dirty, the ocean does not become dirty."

23

"Let the first act of every morning be to make the following resolve for the day:

- I shall not fear anyone on Earth.
- I shall fear only God.
- I shall not bear ill will toward anyone.
- I shall not submit to injustice from anyone.
- I shall conquer untruth by truth. And in resisting untruth, I shall put up with all suffering."

24

"Man often becomes what he believes himself to be. If I keep on saying to myself that I cannot do a certain thing, it is possible that I may end by really becoming incapable of doing it. On the contrary, if I have the belief that I can do it, I shall surely acquire the capacity to do it even if I may not have it at the beginning."

25

"Each night, when I go to sleep, I die. And the next morning, when I wake up, I am reborn."

26

"The greatness of a nation and its moral progress can be judged by the way its animals are treated."

27

"Keep your thoughts positive because your thoughts become your words. Keep your words positive because your words become your behavior. Keep your behavior positive because your behavior becomes your habits. Keep your habits positive because your habits become your values. Keep your values positive because your values become your destiny."

28
"To believe in something, and not to live it, is dishonest."

29
"What difference does it make to the dead, the orphans and the

homeless, whether the mad destruction is wrought under the name of totalitarianism or in the holy name of liberty or democracy?"

30
"There are people in the world so hungry, that God cannot appear to them except in the form of bread."

31
"Whatever you do will be insignificant, but it is very important that you do it."

32
"It is unwise to be too sure of one's own wisdom. It is healthy

to be reminded that the strongest might weaken and the wisest might err."

33
"Truth never damages a cause that is just."

34
"Whenever you are confronted with an opponent. Conquer him with love."

35
"It is easy enough to be friendly to one's friends. But to befriend the one who regards himself as your enemy is the quintessence of true religion. The other is mere business."

36
"Strength does not come from physical capacity. It comes from an indomitable will."

37
"The day the power of love overrules the love of power, the world will know peace."

38
"You don't know who is important to you until you actually lose them."

39
"Action expresses priorities."

40

"You can chain me, you can torture me, you can even destroy this body, but you will never imprison my mind."

41
"I object to violence because when it appears to do good, the good is only temporary; the evil it does is permanent."

42
"My Life is My Message"

43
"You may never know what results come of your actions, but if you do nothing, there will be no results."

44

"What we are doing to the forests of the world is but a mirror reflection of what we are doing to ourselves and to one another."

45

"It's the action, not the fruit of the action, that's important. You have to do the right thing. It may not be in your power, may not be in your time, that there'll be any fruit. But that doesn't mean you stop doing the right thing. You may never know what results come from your action. But if you do nothing, there will be no result."

46

"There is more to life than simply increasing its speed."

47
"Love is the strongest force the world possesses and yet it is the humblest imaginable."

48
"I offer you peace. I offer you love. I offer you friendship. I see your beauty. I hear your need. I feel your feelings."

49
"There is nothing that wastes the body like worry, and one who has any faith in God should be ashamed to worry about anything whatsoever. "

50

"If I had no sense of humor, I would long ago have committed suicide."

51

"The Roots of Violence: Wealth without work, Pleasure without conscience, Knowledge without character, Commerce without morality, Science without humanity, Worship without sacrifice, Politics without principles."

52

"To call woman the weaker sex is a libel; it is man's injustice to woman. If by strength is meant brute strength, then, indeed, is woman less brute than man. If by strength is meant moral power, then woman is immeasurably man's superior. Has she not greater intuition, is she not more self-sacrificing, has she not greater powers of endurance, has she not greater courage? Without her, man could not be. If nonviolence is the law of our being, the future is with woman. Who can make a more effective appeal to the heart than woman?"

53
"There is no 'way to peace,' there is only 'peace."

54

"They cannot take away our self respect if we do not give it to them."

55

"In doing something, do it with love or never do it at all."

56

"Truth is one, paths are many."

57

"I believe in the fundamental truth of all great religions of the world."

58

"A coward is incapable of exhibiting love; it is the prerogative of the brave."

59

"The simplest acts of kindness are by far more powerful then a thousand heads bowing in prayer."

60

"To my mind, the life of a lamb is no less precious than that of a human being."

61

"My imperfections and failures are as much a blessing from God as my successes and my talents and I lay them both at his feet."

62

"I cannot conceive of a greater loss than the loss of one's self-respect."

63

"Always aim at complete harmony of thought and word and deed. Always aim at purifying your thoughts and everything will be well."

64

"Faith is not something to grasp, it is a state to grow into."

65

"Remember that all through history, there have been tyrants

and murderers, and for a time, they seem invincible. But in the end, they always fall. Always."

66
"In a gentle way, you can shake the world."

67
"I believe in equality for everyone, except reporters and photographers."

68
"Power is of two kinds. One is obtained by the fear of punishment and the other by acts of love. Power based on love is a thousand times more effective and permanent than the one

derived from fear of
punishment."

69
"A 'No' uttered from the deepest
conviction is better than a 'Yes'
merely uttered to please, or
worse, to avoid trouble."

70
"I came to the conclusion long
ago that all religions were true
and that also that all had some
error in them, and while I hold by
my own religion, I should hold
other religions as dear as
Hinduism. So we can only pray, if
we were Hindus, not that a
Christian should become a
Hindu; but our innermost prayer

should be that a Hindu should become a better Hindu, a Muslim a better Muslim, and a Christian a better Christian."

71

"Poverty is the worst form of violence."

72

"Silence becomes cowardice when occasion demands speaking out the whole truth and acting accordingly."

73

"I call him religious who understands the suffering of others."

74

"The expert knows more and more about less and less until he knows everything about nothing."

75

"(When asked what he thought of Western civilization): 'I think it would be a good idea."

76

"If we are to reach real peace in the world, we shall have to begin with the children."

77

"There is no school equal to a decent home and no teacher equal to a virtuous parent."

78

"I want freedom for the full expression of my personality."

79

"It is easier to build a boy than to mend a man."

80

"When every hope is gone, 'when helpers fail and comforts flee,' I find that help arrives somehow, from I know not where. Supplication, worship, prayer are no superstition; they are acts more real than the acts of eating, drinking, sitting or walking. It is no exaggeration to say that they alone are real, all else is unreal."

81

"Prayer is not an old woman's idle amusement. Properly understood and applied, it is the most potent instrument of action."

82

"There are many causes I would die for. There is not a single cause I would kill for."

83

"Each one has to find his peace from within. And peace to be real must be unaffected by outside circumstances."

84

"Nothing is so aggravating as calmness."

85
"Nonviolence is a weapon of the strong."

86
"What barrier is there that love cannot break?"

87
"There is force in the universe, which, if we permit it, will flow through us and produce miraculous results."

88

"It is wrong and immoral to seek to escape the consequences of one's acts."

89
"The difference between what we do and what we are capable of doing would suffice to solve most of the world's problems."

90
"Palestine belongs to the Arabs in the same sense that England belongs to the English or France to the French. It is wrong and inhuman to impose the Jews on the Arabs... Surely it would be a crime against humanity to reduce the proud Arabs so that Palestine can be restored to the

Jews partly or wholly as their national home"

91
"There is no such thing as 'too insane' unless others turn up dead due to your actions."

92
"I cannot teach you violence, as I do not myself believe in it. I can only teach you not to bow your heads before any one even at the cost of your life."

93
"Fearlessness is the first requisite of spirituality. Cowards can never be moral."

94

"Yes I am, I am also a Muslim, a Christian, a Buddhist, and a Jew."

95

"I must say that, beyond occasionally exposing me to laughter, my constitutional shyness has been no dis-advantage whatever. In fact I can see that, on the contrary, it has been all to my advantage. My hesitancy in speech, which was once an annoyance, is now a pleasure. Its greatest benefit has been that it has taught me the economy of words. I have naturally formed the habit of restraining my thoughts. And I can now give myself the certificate that a thoughtless word hardly ever escapes my tongue or pen. I do not recollect ever having had to regret anything in my speech or writing. I have thus been spared many a mishap and waste of time. Experience has taught me that silence is part of the spiritual discipline of a votary of truth. Proneness to exaggerate, to suppress or modify the truth, wittingly or unwittingly, is a natural weakness of man, and silence is necessary in order to surmount it. A man of few words will rarely be thoughtless in his speech; he will measure every word. We find so many people impatient to talk. There is no chairman of a meeting who is not pestered with notes for permission to speak. And whenever the permission is given the speaker generally exceeds the time-limit, asks for more time, and keeps on talking without permission. All this talking can hardly be said to be of any benefit to the world. It is so much waste of time. My shyness has been in reality my shield and buckler. It has allowed me to grow. It has helped me in my discernment of truth."

96
"Live simply so that others may simply live."

97
"You can't shake hands with a clenched fist."

98
"The path is the goal."

99
"Liberty and democracy become unholy when their hands are dyed red with innocent blood."

100
"The inner voice is something which cannot be described in words. But sometimes we have a positive feeling that something in us prompts us to do a certain thing. The time when I learnt to recognise this voice was, I may

say, the time when I started
praying regularly."

101

"Carefully watch your thoughts,
for they become your words.
Manage and watch your words,
for they will become your
actions. Consider and judge your
actions, for they have become
your habits. Acknowledge and
watch your habits, for they shall
become your values. Understand
and embrace your values, for
they become your destiny."

102

"Manliness consists not in bluff,
bravado or loneliness. It consists
in daring to do the right thing

and facing consequences
whether it is in matters social,
political or other. It consists in
deeds not words."

103

"The only tyrant I accept in this
world is the 'still small voice'
within me. And even though I
have to face the prospect of being
a minority of one, I humbly
believe I have the courage to be
in such a hopeless minority."

104

"The greatness of humanity is
not in being human, but in being
humane."

105

"Ethically they had arrived at the conclusion that man's supremacy over lower animals meant not that the former should prey upon the latter, but that the higher should protect the lower, and that there should be mutual aid between the two as between man and man. They had also brought out the truth that man eats not for enjoyment but to live."

106

"The seeker after truth should be humbler than the dust. The world crushes the dust under its feet, but the seeker after truth should so humble himself that even the dust could crush him.

Only then, and not till then, will he have a glimpse of truth."

107
"Nothing has saddened me so much in life as the hardness of heart of educated people."

108
"Honest differences are often a healthy sign of progress."

109
"They may torture my body, break my bones, even kill me. Then they will have my dead body, but not my obedience."

110

"Speak only if it improves upon the silence."

111
"Love never claims, it ever gives. Love ever suffers, never resents never revenges itself."

112
"Happiness is when what you think, what you say and what you do are in harmony."

113
"A customer is the most important visitor on our premises. He is not dependent on us. We are dependent on him. He is not an interruption in our work. He is the purpose of it. He

is not an outsider in our business. He is part of it. We are not doing him a favor by serving him. He is doing us a favor by giving us an opportunity to do so."

114
"True beauty lies in purity of the heart."

115
"I become more than ever convinced that it was not the sword that won a place for Islam in those days. It was the rigid simplicity, the utter self-effacement of Hussein, the scrupulous regard for pledges, his intense devotion to his

friends and followers and his intrepidity, his fearlessness, his absolute trust in God and in his own mission. These and not the sword carried everything before them and surmounted every obstacle."

116

"I am but a poor struggling soul yearning to be wholly good, wholly truthful and wholly non-violent in thought, word and deed, but ever failing to reach the ideal which I know to be true. It is a painful climb, but each step upwards makes me feel stronger and fit for the next. "

117

"My grandfather once told me that there were two kinds of people; those who do the work and those who take the credit. He told me to try to be in the first group; there was much less competition."

118
"Wherever you are you will always be in my heart."

119
"No one can ride on the back of a man unless it is bent."

120
"I should love to satisfy all, if I possibly can; but in trying to satisfy all, I may be able to satisfy

none. I have, therefore, arrived at the conclusion that the best course is to satisfy one's own conscience and leave the world to form its own judgment, favorable or otherwise."

121
"The moment there is suspicion about a person's motives, everything he does becomes tainted."

122
"The only difference between man and man all the world over is one of degree, and not of kind, even as there is between trees of the same species.

Where in is the cause for anger, envy or discrimination?"

123
"It is not that I do not get angry. I don't give vent to my anger. I cultivate the quality of patience as angerlessness, and generally speaking, I succeed. But I only control my anger when it comes. How I find it possible to control it would be a useless question, for it is a habit that everyone must cultivate and must succeed in forming by constant practice."

124
"Where love is, there God is also."

125

"Truth resides in every human heart,
and one has to search for it there,
and to be guided by truth as one sees it.
But no one has a right to coerce others
to act according to his own view of truth."

126
"If I were asked to define the Hindu creed, I should simply say: Search after truth through non-violent means. A man may not believe in God and still call himself a Hindu. Hinduism is a relentless pursuit after truth... Hinduism is the religion of truth. Truth is God. Denial of God we

have known. Denial of truth we
have not known."

127
"Non-violence, which is the
quality of the heart, cannot come
by an appeal to the brain."

128
"Where there is life, there is
love."

129
"Prayer is the key of the morning
and the bolt of the evening."

130
"There would be nothing to
frighten you if you refused to be
afraid."

131

"it's easy to stand in the crowd but it takes courage to stand alone"

132

"Every worthwhile accomplishment, big or little, has its stages of drudgery and triumph: a beginning, a struggle, and a victory."

133

"If I have the belief that I can do it, I shall surely acquire the capacity to do it even if I may not have it at the beginning."

134

"Champions are made from something they have deep inside of them-a desire, a dream, a vison."

135
"Satisfaction lies in the effort, not in the attainment."

136
"It is good to see ourselves as others see us. Try as we may, we are never
able to know ourselves fully as we are, especially the evil side of us.
This we can do only if we are not angry with our critics but will take in good heart whatever they might have to say."

137

"I have learnt through bitter experience the one supreme lesson to conserve my anger, and as heat conserved is transmuted into energy, even so our anger controlled can be transmuted into a power which can move the world."

138

"True love is boundless like the ocean and, swelling within one, spreads itself out and, crossing all boundaries and frontiers, envelops the whole world."

139

"It is better to be violent, if there is violence in our hearts, than to put on the cloak of nonviolence to cover impotence."

140
"Everyone holds a piece of the truth."

141
"If you don't find God in the next person you meet, it is a waste of time looking for him further."

142
"To believe that what has not occurred in history will not occur at all, is to argue disbelief in the dignity of man."

143
"You yourself as much as anybody in the entire universe deserve love and affection."

144
"If I were a dictator, religion and state would be separate. I swear by my religion. I will die for it. But it is my personal affair. The state has nothing to do with it. The state would look after your secular welfare, health, communications, foreign relations, currency and so on, but not your or my religion. That is everybody's personal concern!"

145

"The only tyrant I accept is the still, small voice within me."

146
"Service which is rendered without joy helps neither the servant nor the served. But all other pleasures and possessions pale into nothingness before service which is rendered in a spirit of joy."

147
"To forgive is not to forget. The merit lies in loving in spite of the vivid knowledge that one that must be loved is not a friend. There is not merit in loving an enemy when you forget him for a friend. "

148

"The golden rule of conduct is mutual toleration, seeing that we will never all think alike and we shall always see Truth in fragment and from different points of vision."

149

"Satisfaction lies in the effort, not in the attainment. Full effort is full victory."

150

"I first learned the concepts of non-violence in my marriage."

151

"The various religions

are like different roads
converging on the same point.
What difference does it make
if we follow different routes,
provided we arrive
at the same destination?"

152
"Hatred can be overcome only by
love. "

153
"I may be a despicable person,
but when Truth speaks through
me I am
invincible."

154
"As human beings, our greatness
lies not so much in being able to

remake the world - that is the myth of the atomic age - as in being able to remake ourselves."

155
"The world has enough for everyone's need, but not enough for everyone's greed."

156
"There goes my people. I must follow them, for I am their leader."

157
"A man, whilst he is dreaming, believes in his dream; he is undeceived only when he is awakened from his slumber."

158

"Even if you are a minority of one, the Truth is the Truth."

159

"An ounce of practice is worth more than tons of preaching."

160

"If you're going to be a bear, be a grizzly."

161

"Terrorism and deception are weapons not of the strong, but of the weak."

162

"An unjust law is itself a species of violence. Arrest for its breach is more so. Now the law of nonviolence says that violence should be resisted not by counter-violence but by nonviolence. This I do by breaking the law and by peacefully submitting to arrest and imprisonment."

163
"And when Hugh would grow progressively Gandhi on me, I'd remind him that these were pests---disease carriers who feasted upon the dead and then came indoors to dance upon our silverware."

164

"An error does not become truth by reason of multiplied propagation, nor does the truth become error because nobody will see it."

165
"Don't talk about it. The rose doesn't have to propagate its perfume. It just gives it forth, and people are drawn to it. Live it, and people will come to see the source of your power."

166
"In the attitude of silence the soul finds the path in a clearer light, and what is elusive and deceptive resolves itself into crystal clearness. Our life is a

long and arduous quest after
Truth. "

167

"But no one has a right to coerce
others to act according to his
own view of truth."

168

"The law of love could be best
understood and learned through
little children."

169

"True morality consists not in
following the beaten track, but in
finding the true path for
ourselves, and fearlessly
following it."

170

"A small body of determined spirits fired by an unquenchable faith in their mission can alter the course of history."

171

"Victory attained by violence is tantamount to a defeat for it is momentary."

172

"Compassion is a muscle that gets stronger with use."

173

"All your scholarship would be in vain if at the same time you do not build your character and

attain mastery over your
thoughts and your actions."

174
"In matters of conscience, the
law of the majority has no place."

175
"Peace between countries must
rest on the solid foundation of
love between individuals."

176
"Birth and death are not two
different states, but they are
different aspects of the same
state."

177

"The more efficient a force is, the more silent and the more subtle it is."

178

"Of all the evils for which man has made himself responsible, none is so degrading, so shocking or so brutal as his abuse of the better half of humanity; the female sex."

179

"One man cannot do right in one department of life whilst he is occupied in doing wrong in any other department. Life is one indivisible whole"

180

"What lies ahead of you & what lies behind you is nothing compared to what lies within you."

181
"Recall the face of the poorest and weakest man you have seen, and ask yourself if this step you contemplate is going to be any use to him."

182
"A man of character will make himself worthy of any position he is given."

183

"A language is an exact reflection of the character and growth of its speakers."

184
"I claim to be no more than the average person with less than average ability. I have not the shadow of a doubt that any man or woman can achieve what I have, if he or she would make the same effort and cultivate the same hope and faith."

185
"Cowardice is impotence worse than violence. The coward desires revenge but being afraid to die, he looks to others, maybe to the government of the day, to

do the work of defense for him. A coward is less than a man. He does not deserve to be a member of a society of men and women."

186
"Do not crave to know the views of others, nor base your intent thereon. To think independently for yourself is a sign of fearlessness."

187
"Where there is fear there is no religion."

188
"The power to question is the basis of all human progress."

189

"A religion that takes no account of practical affairs and does not help to solve them is no religion."

190

"Among the many misdeeds of British rule in India, history will look upon the Act which deprived a whole nation of arms as the blackest."

191

"But you can wake a man only if he is really asleep. No effort that you make will produce any effect upon him if he is merely pretending sleep."

192

"It is man's social nature which distinguishes him from the brute creation. If it is his privilege to be independent, it is equally his duty to be inter-dependent. Only an arrogant man will claim to be independent of everybody else and be self-contained."

193
"If you want something really important to be done you must not merely satisfy the reason, you must move the heart also."

194
"Men often become what they believe themselves to be. If I believe I cannot do something,it

makes me incapable of doing it.
When I believe I can,I acquire
the ability to do it even if I didn't
have it in the beginning.'"

195
"I offer you peace.
I offer you love.
I offer you friendship.
I see your beauty.
I hear your need.
I feel your feelings.
My wisdom flows from the
highest Source.
I salute that Source in you.
Let us work together. For unity
and peace."

196

"Behaviour is the mirror in which we can display our image."

197
"There are two days in the year that we can not do anything, yesterday and tomorrow"

198
"You can't lead a true life without suffering"

199
"An unjust law is itself a species of violence. Arrest for its breach is more so."

200
"Sacrifice is joy."

201

"I have also seen children successfully surmounting the effects of an evil inheritance. That is due to purity being an inherent attribute of the soul."

202

"One needs to be slow to form convictions, but once formed they must be defended against the heaviest odds."

203

"Truth has drawn me into the field of politics; and I can say without the slightest hesitation, and yet in all humility, that those who say that religion has nothing to do with politics do not know what religion means."

204
"Love is the strongest force the world possesses."

205
"As long as you derive inner help and comfort from anything, keep it."

206
"There's no God higher than truth."

207
"I shall die, but I will not kill."

208

"You Christians look after a document containing enough dynamite to blow all civilization to pieces, turn the world upside down and bring peace to a battle-torn planet. But you treat it as though it is nothing more than a piece of literature."

209
"Strength of numbers is the delight of the timid. The Valiant in spirit glory in fighting alone."

210
"Non-violence is the greatest force at the disposal of mankind. It is mightier than the mightiest weapon of destruction devised by the ingenuity of man."

211

"I do not want my house to be walled in on all sides and my windows to be stuffed. I want the culture of all lands to be blown about my house as freely as possible. But I refuse to be blown off my feet by any"

212

"In fact, it is more correct to say that Truth is God, than to say that God is Truth."

213

"I have naturally formed the habit of restraining my thoughts. A thoughtless word hardly ever escaped my tongue or pen.

Experience has taught me that silence is part of the spiritual discipline of a votary of truth. We find so many people impatient to talk. All this talking can hardly be said to be of any benefit to the world. It is so much waste of time. My shyness has been in reality my shield and buckler. It has allowed me to grow. It has helped me in my discernment of truth."

214
"Anger and intolerance are the twin enemies of correct understanding."

215

"No culture can live, if it attempts to be exclusive."

216
"A man who is truthful and does not mean ill even to his adversary will be slow to believe charges even against his foes. He will, however, try to understand the viewpoints of his opponents and will always keep an open mind and seek every opportunity of serving his opponents."

217
"My effort should never be to undermine another's faith but to make him a better follower of his own faith."

218

"A weak man is just by accident. A strong but non-violent man is unjust by accident."

219

"Stoning prophets and erecting churches to their memory afterwards has been the way of the world through the ages. Today we worship Christ, but the Christ in the flesh we crucified."

220

"It is also a warning. It is a warning that, if nobody reads the writing on the wall, man will be reduced to the state of the beast, whom he is shaming by his manners."

221

"I can retain neither respect nor affection for government which has been moving from wrong to wrong in order to defend its immorality"

222

"Forgiveness is a virtue of the brave."

223

"One thing we have endeavoured to observe most scrupulously, namely, never to depart from the strictest facts and, in dealing with the difficult questions that have arisen during the year, we hope that we have used the utmost moderation possible under the circumstances."

224

"Our duty is very simple and plain. We want to serve the community, and in our own humble way to serve the Empire. We believe in the righteousness of the cause, which it is our privilege to espouse. We have an abiding faith in the mercy of the Almighty God, and we have firm faith in the British Constitution. That being so, we should fail in our duty if we wrote anything with a view to hurt."

225

"Facts we would always place before our readers, whether they are palatable or not, and it is by placing them constantly before the public in their nakedness that the misunderstanding between the two communities in South Africa can be removed."

226
"Distinguish between real needs and artificial wants and control the latter."

227
"I am prepared to die, but there is no cause for which I am prepared to kill."

228

"Sympathy is what you have for someone after they die, pity you have for someone when they don't have a date to the biggest dance of the year. Empathy is what I do to you when you judge me. Envy is having pity on yourself. Can you discern the rest for yourself?"

229
"Just as a man would not cherish living in a body other than his own, so do nations not like to live under other nations, however noble and great the latter may be."

230

"I look upon an increase in the power of the State with the greatest fear because, although while apparently doing good by minimizing exploitation, it does the greatest harm to mankind by destroying individuality which lies at the heart of all progress."

231
"The devotion of such titans of spirit as Lenin to an Ideal must bear fruit. The nobility of his selflessness will be an example through centuries to come, and his Ideal will reach perfection."

232
"We do not need to proselytise either by our speech or by our

writing. We can only do so really with our lives. Let our lives be open books for all to study."

233

"I appeal for cessation of hostilities, not because you are too exhausted to fight, but because war is bad in essence. You want to kill Nazism. You will never kill it by its indifferent adoption."

234

"Freedom is not worth having if it does not connote freedom to err. It passes my comprehension how human beings, be they ever so experienced and able, can delight in depriving other human beings of that precious right."

235
"I believe in trusting. Trust begets trust. Suspicion is fetid and only stinks. He who trusts has never yet lost in the world."

236
"Human language can but imperfectly describe God's ways. I am sensible of the fact that they are indescribable and inscrutable. But if mortal man will dare to describe them, he has no better medium than his own inarticulate speech."

237

"Intellect takes us along in the battle of life to a certain limit, but at the crucial moment it fails us. Faith transcends reason. It is when the horizon is the darkest and human reason is beaten down to the ground that faith shines brightest and comes to our rescue."

238
"We stand on the threshold of a twilight-whether morning or evening we do not know. One is followed by the night, the other heralds the dawn."

239

"In prayer it is better to have a heart without words than words without a heart."

240
"Joy lies in the fight, in the attempt, in the suffering involved, not in the victory itself"

241
"I do not believe in the doctrine of the greatest good of the greatest number. The only real, dignified, human doctrine is the greatest good of all."

242
"Civilization is the encouragement of differences."

243
"You must learn to be still in the midst of activity and vibrantly alive in repose."

244
"That service is the noblest which is rendered for its own sake."

245
"Intolerance betrays want of faith in one's cause."

246
"There are only two ways to live your life: as though nothing is a miracle, or as though everything is a miracle."

247
"We should be able to refuse to live if the price of living be the torture of sentient beings."

248
"Government control gives rise to fraud, suppression of Truth, intensification of the black market and artificial scarcity. Above all, it unmans the people and deprives them of initiative, it undoes the teaching of self-help..."

249
"All true artists, whether they know it or not, create from a place of no-mind, from inner stillness."

250

"Hatred ever kills, love never dies. Such is the vast difference between the two. What is obtained by love is retained for all time. What is obtained by hatred proves a burden in reality for it increases hatred."

251

"Truth should be the very breath of our life. When once this state in the pilgrim's progress is reached, all other rules of correct living will come without any effort, and obedience to them will be instinctive."

252

"Every home is a university and the parents are the teachers."

253
"I offer you peace. I offer you love. I offer you friendship. I see your beauty. I hear your need. I feel your feelings. My wisdom flows from the Highest Source. I salute that Source in you. Let us work together for unity and love."

254
"First they ignore you, then they laugh at you, then they fight you, then you win."

255

"Even the most despotic government cannot stand except for the consent of the governed.... Immediately the subject ceases to fear the despotic force, his power is gone."

256

"God, as Truth, has been for me a treasure beyond price. May He be so to every one of us."

257

"Interdependence is and ought to be as much the ideal of man as self-sufficiency. Man is a social being. Without interrelation with society he cannot realize his oneness with the universe or suppress his egotism. His social interdependence enables him to test his faith and to prove himself on the touchstone of reality."

258
"All humanity is one undivided and indivisible family. I cannot detach myself from the wickedest soul."

259
"Truth is like a vast tree which yields more and more fruit the more you nurture it. The deeper the search in the mind of truth, the richer the discovery of the gems buried there."

260

"We but mirror the world. All the tendencies present in the outer world are to be found in the world of our body. If we could change ourselves, the tendencies in the world would also change. As a man changes his own nature, so does the attitude of the world change towards him. This is the divine mystery supreme. A wonderful thing it is and the source of our happiness. We need not wait to see what others do."

261

"This is my country, that is your country, these are the conceptions of narrow souls, to the liberal minded the whole world is a family"

262
"Morality is a contraband in war."

263
"Human beings, who are almost unique in having the ability to learn from the experience of others, are also remarkable for their apparent disinclination to do so.

You must not lose faith in humanity. Humanity is an ocean if a few drops of the ocean are dirty, the ocean does not become dirty."

— Mahatma Gandhi

264

"Strength does not come from physical capacity. It comes from an indomitable will."

265

"[I]t seems to me as clear as daylight that abortion would be a crime."

266

"If we are to make progress, we must not repeat history but make new history. We must add to inheritance left by our ancestors."

267

"I crave to die with my hand at the spinning wheel."
— Mahatma Gandhi

268
"The meek may one day inherit the earth, but not the headlines."

269
"Non-cooperation with evil is as much a duty as is cooperation with good."

270
"The weak can never forgive. Forgiveness is the attribute of the strong.

271

"I was a coward. I used to be haunted by the fear of thieves, ghosts and serpents. I did not dare to stir out of doors at night. Darkness was a terror to me. It was almost impossible for me to sleep in the dark, as I would imagine ghosts coming from one direction, thieves from another and serpents from a third. I could not therefore bear to sleep without a light in the room. "
― Mahatma Gandhi

272
"Hesitating to act because the whole vision might not be achieved, or because others do not yet share it, is an attitude that only hinders progress."

273

"It has always been a mystery to me how men can feel themselves honored by the humiliation of their fellow beings."

274

"All have not the same capacity. I would allow a man of intellect to earn more, I would not cramp his talent."

275

"There are as many different religions as there are individuals."

276

"Gentleness, self-sacrifice and generosity are the exclusive possession of no one race or religion."

277
"Love is the subtlest force in the world."

278
"The Best Thing To Find Yourself Is To Loose Yourself In The Service Of Others"

279
"Every known thief pretends to be a gentleman at first!"

280

"Whenever you are in doubt, or when the self becomes too much with you, apply the following test. Recall the face of the poorest and the weakest man whom you may have seen, and ask yourself if the step you contemplate is going to be of any use to him. Will he gain anything by it? Will it restore him to a control over his own life and destiny? In other words, will it lead to swaraj for the hungry and spiritually starving millions?"

281
"We don't use guns because we don't have guns"

282

"Men often become what they believe themselves to be.If I believe I cannot do something,it makes me incapable of doing it. But when I believe I can , then I acquire the ability to do it even If I didn't have it in the beginning"."

283

"I too took the plunge - the vow to observe brahmacharya for life. I must confess that I had not then fully realized the magnitude and immensity of the task I undertook. The difficulties are even today staring me in the face. The importance of the vow is being more and more borne in upon me. Life without brahmacharya appears to me to be insipid and animal-like. The brute by nature knows no self-restraint. Man is man because he is capable of, and only in so far as he exercises, self-restraint. What formerly appeared to me to be extravagant praise of brahmacharya in our religious books seems now, with increasing clearness every day, to be absolutely proper and founded on experience."

284

"A vow is a purely religious act which cannot be taken in a fit of passion. It can be taken with a mind purified and composed and with God as witness."

285

"I have not conceived my mission to be that of a knight-errant wandering everywhere to deliver people from difficult situations. My humble occupation has been to show people how they can solve their own difficulties."

286

"I believe that just as everyone inherits a particular form so does he inherit the particular characteristics and qualities of his progenitors, and to make this admission is to conserve one's energy."

287

"And whilst he may not claim superiority by reason of learning, I myself must not withold that meed of homage that learning, wherever it resides, always commands."

288
"unity to be real must survive the severest strain without breaking."

289
"Those who say religion has nothing to do with politics do not know what religion is."

290
"The good man is the friend of all living things."

291

"Truth is transcendent. There are many expressions of it and ways to glimpse it. We cannot hold it in our clenched fist, but must hold it in our open palm and invite others to see it for themselves."

292

"I might be ready to embrace a snake, but, if one comes to bite you, I should kill it and protect you."

293

"Good travels at a snail's pace. Those who want to do good are not selfish, they are not in a hurry, they know that to impregnate people with good requires a long time."

294

"We must be ever courteous and patient with those who do not see eye to eye with us. We must resolutely refuse to consider our opponents as enemies."

295

"The future depends on what we do in the present."

296

"The history of the world is full of men who rose to leadership, by sheer force of self-confidence, bravery and tenacity."

297
"The more you try to run away from something, in reality, the more you are nearing it!"

298
"My life is my message."

299
"I'm a lover of my own liberty, and so I would do nothing to restrict yours."

300
"Religion which takes no account of practical affairs and does not help to solve them is no religion."

Also by Daniel Willey:

365 Fun, Uplifting, Motivating, and Inspirational Quotes You've Never Heard Before

365 Fun, Uplifting, and Inspirational Quotes from all the Top Movies

Be Great: 365 Inspirational Quotes from the World's Most Influential People

Success Isn't For Everyone: How to Build the Foundation for a Successful Future

The Top 365 Fun, Uplifting, Motivating, and Inspirational Quotes of all Time

Daily Love Quotes

About The Author

Daniel Willey became interested in books at a very young age. His mother was a huge advocate of reading and would regularly hold 'read-a-thons' for the family. Daniel graduated from the University of Utah in Emergency Medicine. He spent two years as a missionary in Thailand and has a great love for the country and people there. Daniel is currently writing another book and says that he has several ideas for more books "in the pipeline."

Made in the USA
Coppell, TX
09 June 2025

50485344R10067